Indian Nations

THE CHEYENNE

by
Dennis Limberhand and Mary Em Parrilli

General Editors
Herman J. Viola and David Jeffery

A Rivilo Book

RAINTREE
STECK-VAUGHN
PUBLISHERS

A Harcourt Company

Austin · New York
www.steck-vaughn.com

Published by Raintree Steck-Vaughn Company, an imprint of the
Steck-Vaughn Company

Developed for Steck-Vaughn Company by Rivilo Books
Editor: David Jeffery
Photo Research: Brenda McLain
Design: Barbara Lisenby and Todd Hirshman
Electronic Preparation: Lyda Guz

Raintree Steck-Vaughn Publishers Staff
Publishing Director: Walter Kossmann
Editor: Kathy DeVico

The Creation Story on pages 5–7 is based on George A. Dorsey's account in 1905.

Photo Credits: Photo Credits: John Warner: cover, pp. 25 top, 30, 31 bottom, 38, 39, 40 top; Lisa Ranallo Horse Capture: illustration, pp. 4, 6, 7; Bates Littlehales/National Geographic Image Collection: p. 9; Yoshi Miyake: illustration, p. 10; National Museum of Natural History, Smithsonian Institution: pp. 11, 21, 22 top, 23 right, 24, 25 bottom right, 35 top right and bottom right; National Anthropological Archives, Smithsonian Institution: pp. 13 top, 15, 16 top, 18, 20, 22 bottom, 23 bottom, 27, 29, 31 top, 32, 34; Denver Public Library: p. 13 bottom; Herman Viola: pp. 14, 26, 28, 36, 45; Little Bighorn National Battlefield Monument Museum: p. 16 bottom; Woolaroc Museum, Bartlesville, Oklahoma: p. 17; National Museum of the American Indian, Smithsonian Institution: p. 35 middle left; Brenda McLain: p. 40 bottom; Ric Ergenbright/Corbis: p. 42.

Library of Congress Cataloging-in-Publication Data
Limberhand, Dennis
    The Cheyenne / by Dennis Limberhand and Mary Em Parrilli
      p. cm. — (Indian nations)
    Includes bibliographical references and index.
    ISBN 0-8172-5469-2
    1. Cheyenne Indians — History — Juvenile literature. 2. Cheyenne
Indians — Social life and customs — Juvenile literature. [1. Cheyenne
Indians. 2. Indians of North America — Great Plains.] I. Parrilli, Mary Em.
II. Title. III. Indian nations (Austin, Tex.)
E99.C53 L543 2001
978.004'973—dc21

                    00-034160

Printed and bound in the United States
1 2 3 4 5 6 7 8 9 0 LB 04 03 02 01 00

Cover photo: A Northern Cheyenne boy, dressed as a traditional warrior, is ready to take part in a powwow.

Contents

Pronunciation of some Cheyenne words are found in the Glossary.

Creation Story

In the beginning, the Great Medicine created the land, the waters, the Sun, and the Moon. Then he made a beautiful country in the far north.

Into this country the Great Medicine put four-legged animals, birds, insects, fish, and creatures of all kinds. Then he created human beings to live with the creatures. Every animal, big and small, every bird, every fish, and every insect could talk to the people in a common language. They all lived together in friendship. The people lived simply, and they were never hungry. They wandered among the wild animals. At night they lay on the cool earth and slept. During the days they talked with the animals, and all were friends.

The Great Medicine created human beings. First, he made those who had hair all over their bodies. Second, he created white men who had hair on their heads, faces, and legs. Finally, he made red men who had long hair only on their heads. The hairy people were strong and active. The white people were powerful and intelligent. The red people were swift and graceful runners. The Great Medicine taught them all how to fish and hunt.

After a while the hairy people left the North Country and went south to a barren land. The red people prepared to follow them, but before they could do so, the Great Medicine called the red people all together. He blessed them and gave the red

◀ *The Great Medicine took pity on the red men, who had traveled far and suffered much. He gave them corn to plant and buffalo to eat.*

5

people special medicine spirits to open their minds. From that time on, they possessed intelligence and always knew what to do. Great Medicine called one man and told him to band the people together so that they could work as a group. He told them to clothe their bodies with animal skins. He gave them the power to shape rocks and other stones into many things, such as spear points, knives, and axes.

The red people stayed together after that. When they arrived in the South, they found that the hairy people had scattered and were living in caves in the hills and mountains. The red people seldom saw the hairy people. Eventually the hairy people disappeared entirely from the face of the Earth.

After the disappearance of the hairy people, Great Medicine told the red men to return to the North, because the lands of the South would soon be flooded. When the red people returned to the North, they found the white-skinned, long-bearded men were gone. Some of the wild animals had also disappeared, and the red people found that they were no longer able to communicate with other creatures.

Then for the second time the red people were told to leave the beautiful northlands and go south. The South was now a beautiful land, but a flood came and the people nearly starved.

The red men returned north, but they found the land there was barren and dry. The men were sad, and the women and children cried. These things happened in the very beginning.

Finally the people returned south again. They continued to live there for hundreds of years. Then the Earth shook, and the hills sent forth fire and smoke. The winter was long and cold and destroyed the trees. The red men suffered a great deal. Finally, the Great Medicine took pity on them. He gave them corn to plant and buffalo to eat. The people continued to live in the South, but now there were many different bands with many different languages. The red men were never again united.

The Wonderful Bundle

A very long time ago, a man named Wolf Moon was living by himself in a lodge. He did not have any family or relatives. He ate roots and berries and meat that he had dried and wore clothing from the animals that he had skinned.

One day a man called Wihio (ve-HEE-oh)—a white man like a spider whom the Great Medicine had made—stopped by Wolf Moon's lodge. Wihio said: "I am glad that I have found you, my brother. I have been looking for you for a long time, and I have asked everyone where you live. At last I learned where your lodge was, so I came straight to you."

After greeting Wihio, Wolf Moon began to cook dinner for them. While Wolf Moon was cooking, Wihio began to look around the lodge. He saw a large bundle tied to a tripod made of three poles. He wondered what power or medicine that it might have in it. He grew more and more curious, but was never able to examine the bundle's contents.

After dinner, Wihio said to Wolf Moon, "My brother, may I sleep here tonight?" Wolf Moon said that he could stay, and they made up their beds. Wolf Moon had seen Wihio looking at the bundle and thought that he might be planning to steal it. Soon they went to bed, but Wihio did not sleep. He lay awake watching and waiting. When Wolf Moon finally fell asleep, Wihio got up and untied the bundle. He put it on his back and carried it out of the lodge.

After walking a long way, Wihio reached a lake and began to run along the shore. He ran all night along the lakeshore, which seemed to have no end. After a while, he became very tired and lay down to rest with the bundle still on his back.

In the morning when Wolf Moon awoke, he saw Wihio lying there with his head on the bundle. Wolf Moon said to him, "My brother, what are you doing with my bundle?"

Wihio awakened to find himself still in the lodge. Upon realizing that the running had all been a dream, he said, "My brother, you have treated me so nicely that I was going to guard and protect your bundle for you."

After they ate breakfast, Wihio asked Wolf Moon what he was afraid of. Wolf Moon answered, "My brother, I am afraid of nothing except a goose." Wihio responded that he also feared geese and regarded them as very frightening birds. Wihio then thanked Wolf Moon and told him that he was going home.

That night Wihio came back to the lodge in the shape of a goose. Wihio called out loudly and so frightened Wolf Moon that he put his bundle on his back and ran out. Then Wihio went and got his wife and family and brought them back to the lodge. He told them that they would now have a good home with plenty of food and firewood.

Wihio then told his wife about the bundle. He planned to follow Wolf Moon and find out what was hidden in his bundle.

That evening, after eating dinner, Wihio set out to follow Wolf Moon's trail. He followed it for a long time. When he found Wolf

In the folktale of the wonderful bundle, geese, like this real hissing Canada goose, inspired fear. Wihio used that fear to trick Wolf Moon.

Moon, Wihio called out as a goose to frighten him. Wolf Moon ran away but held on to his bundle. Wihio kept following. Several more times Wihio made the sound of a goose, but each time that Wolf Moon ran away he carried the bundle with him. At last

In the story, buffalo like this one escape one by one. But then Wihio opened his bundle once too often, and he was killed.

he became so tired that he dropped the bundle, and Wihio grabbed it. When Wolf Moon saw what Wihio had done, he warned him to open the bundle only four times.

Wihio returned to the lodge and told his wife that he now had the mysterious bundle and planned to look inside. However, as soon as he opened it, a buffalo ran out, and other buffalo tried to escape. Wihio quickly closed the bundle, keeping the other buffalo inside.

Wihio killed the one buffalo, and his family had plenty of good meat. When they had eaten it all, Wihio opened the bundle a second time and another buffalo jumped out. Again he killed the animal. When this meat was gone, Wihio opened the bundle a third time, but he had forgotten to keep count of the buffalo that he had killed. When he opened the bundle for the fourth time, Wihio thought that he had only done it three times.

When Wihio opened the bundle for the fifth time, he was unable to close it. So many buffalo rushed out that he and his whole family were trampled and killed.

That is the story of where the buffalo came from. From Wolf Moon's bundle they ran north and south and east and west, and spread all over the countryside. But that was the last of Wihio!

Key Historical Events

Before 1700, the Cheyenne lived as farmers in the woodlands of present-day Wisconsin and Minnesota. They lived in earth lodges clustered in permanent villages and were both hunters and farmers. The Cheyenne made beads, figurines, and pottery from clay from the earth, and they also made woven baskets.

The Cheyenne nation's first meeting with real, not mythical, white people occurred in about 1680. That year a group of Cheyenne visited the fort of the French explorer Robert de La Salle. The Cheyenne admired the metal tools, blankets, glass beads, and other attractive things that belonged to the French. They invited the French trappers to their country to trap beaver and other fur-bearing animals and to open a trading post where the Cheyenne could trade for European products.

This Cheyenne breast ornament was made of bone and glass beads. It was collected long ago and shows two artistic traditions: Cheyenne and European.

A little later the Cheyenne were forced to cross the Minnesota River, and eventually migrated into the Black Hills of present-day South Dakota. They probably fled Minnesota because of warfare with their traditional enemies, the **Ojibwa** and the **Assiniboin**, who were more numerous and better armed.

When the Cheyenne reached the Great Plains, their lifestyle changed a lot. The Great Plains of North America contain millions of square miles of bluffs, flat-topped mesas, wooded valleys, streams, and open grasslands. A short, hardy grass called "buffalo grass" then covered much of the grasslands,

11

which were home to millions and millions of buffalo. There the Cheyenne also found horses. After capturing and training horses, the Cheyenne began a new life as nomadic warriors and buffalo hunters. According to their oral history, they "lost the corn," meaning that they no longer planted crops. They also stopped making pottery and baskets because those items broke easily during the people's frequent moves. The Cheyenne started ed using animal skins for clothing and utensils.

The Cheyenne way of life again changed dramatically in the 19th century with the arrival of many white people in their country. The Cheyenne wanted to live peaceably with the white settlers, but this was difficult. The settlers built forts, towns, railroads, roads, and fences that disrupted the movements of the buffalo, which were essential to the well-being of the Cheyenne.

The newcomers also brought with them many diseases to which the Cheyenne and other Indians had no immunity. For example, in 1849 a cholera epidemic wiped out several entire bands of the Cheyenne. The disease killed about 2,000 people—nearly two-thirds of the tribe.

The United States government tried to help the Cheyenne with their concerns about white settlers. It made treaties with the Cheyenne that were supposed to protect their rights and keep them from coming into conflict with the settlers. The treaties provided the Cheyenne with food, clothing, tools, and other goods as a sort of payment for allowing white people to settle on their land.

About 1832 the Cheyenne tribe divided into two groups. One group stayed along the headwaters of the Platte River in what is today eastern Wyoming, northern Colorado, and western Nebraska. They became known as the Northern Cheyenne tribe. This group later became friendly with the Lakota Sioux.

U.S. Commissioners and Indian chiefs gather in council in Wyoming to make the Treaty of Ft. Laramie in 1868. The treaty, signed by Lakotas and Cheyennes, agreed to closing the settlers' trail to goldfields in Montana. It was later broken by the U.S. That led to war on the Plains.

The other group settled farther south near the upper Arkansas River, in what is now eastern Colorado and western Kansas. In 1851 these Southern Cheyenne, along with the Arapaho and other tribes living on the Great Plains, signed the Treaty of Fort Laramie. The intent of the U.S. government in making the treaty was to assure safe travel and protection for white settlers traveling along the Oregon Trail.

But the settlers' horses, cows, and oxen ate all the grass along the trail. As a result, the buffalo and other animals had to go elsewhere to find food. The travelers disrupted animal and human life along the trail and polluted the rivers and streams. Because so

White settlers began to pour into the land of the western Indians after the Civil War. Here wagon trains bound for Oregon come together in 1870 at Wyoming's Red Buttes and the North Platte River.

many settlers used the trail across their lands, the Cheyenne sometimes asked them for a payment or toll of tobacco or sugar. Once in a while when this happened, the white people thought the Indians were attacking them.

For example, in 1856, two Cheyenne warriors near Fort Kearney, Nebraska, approached a mail wagon hoping to get some tobacco. The driver of the wagon sped away and fired his pistol at the Indians. This angered the Indians who then chased the driver and injured him with an arrow. The soldiers at Fort Kearney retaliated with a surprise attack on a nearby Cheyenne village. The soldiers killed eight Cheyenne, took 22 horses, and destroyed the camp. This unfair attack began a war between the Cheyenne and the U.S. cavalry that lasted more than 20 years.

Other brutal incidents followed. Twice the constantly moving village of the Cheyenne Chief Black Kettle was attacked—once in 1864, at Sand Creek, when more than 200 Cheyenne men, women, and children were killed, and again in 1868, at Washita, when another 100 villagers were slaughtered.

Because of the attacks, most of the Southern Cheyenne surrendered and went to live on lands in Indian Territory (present-day Oklahoma). However, the Northern Cheyenne continued to resist. In the summer of 1876, Cheyenne leaders such as Two Moon and Lame White Man, joined forces with their Lakota friends and relatives led by the great spiritual leader

U.S. Senator Ben Nighthorse Campbell, himself a Cheyenne, stands by a marker at Sand Creek. Here the Colorado militia attacked a Cheyenne village in 1864, massacring more than 200.

In 1868 the Cheyenne were again attacked without warning at their encampment on the Washita River. This time it was by troops under Lt. Colonel George Armstrong Custer.

Sitting Bull and the warrior Crazy Horse. These Lakota and the Cheyenne would rather die in battle than live on a **reservation**, which they regarded as little more than a jail. The government labeled these Indians as "hostiles" and ordered the U.S. Army to find them and force them onto reservations.

Meanwhile, the Cheyenne and the Lakota held ceremonies in preparation for forthcoming conflicts. In one ceremony Sitting Bull had a vision predicting the soldiers would be defeated.

The warriors prepared themselves for battle by praying and singing special songs. When leading his men into battle, the great Lakota war chief Crazy Horse would sing, "It is a good day to die, and a good day to fight! Cowards to the rear, brave hearts...follow me!" Warriors also believed they had protective powers received from the Creator. They painted their bodies in beautiful colors and wore decorated war clothes when they went into battle. The warriors also painted their horses with special symbols that they believed made them strong and bulletproof.

Although most warriors were men, some women also went into battle. Some even fought as warriors. When soldiers approached Sitting Bull's village in mid-June 1876, Crazy Horse led a large number of Cheyenne and Lakota warriors in an attempt

to stop them. For six hours the Indians and soldiers fought a fierce battle along the banks of Rosebud Creek in Montana.

A medical doctor, Thomas B. Marquis (left), lived among the Cheyenne and interviewed many. Here he talks to Wooden Leg, who described the Battle of the Rosebud and drew a picture of some of the action in it (below). The battle was fought a week before the struggle at Little Bighorn.

Pencil writing by Ben Shoulderblade, a school-educated Cheyenne Indian.

Drawn by Wooden Leg — 1930

Richard Wooden Leg save the man when he was just about kill by the enemy.

296

Wooden Leg making this drawing. —1930.

Page 202, "A Warrior Who Fought Custer."

At battle of the Rosebud, June 17, 1876, Wooden Leg rescued Black Sun, a wounded Cheyenne. Black Sun died that night, in camp.

Blood gushing out from Black Sun's left side, to ground. Costumes and general makeup of each warrior just as it was at time of battle. Bridles, horse-blankets, guns, etc., same. Note that Wooden Leg has only a revolver (cap-and-ball) as his weapon. Black Sun has a rifle.

The warriors prepared themselves for this battle, so the tails of their horses are tied up.

Many horsetracks indicate much movement of horsemen there at that time. Imagination must supply to fill the scene. Note special tracks of Wooden Leg's horse far left to far right, as he had gone to get his wounded fellow warrior.

See the bullets flying past them, going toward left. Bullets represented by short pencil-lines nubbed at ends.

Called "Custer's Last Fight," this painting is rare for showing the battle from the Indians' point of view. Many of the Indian warriors were armed with repeating rifles. The troops with Custer were armed with single-shot rifles.

With the Cheyenne that day was Buffalo-Calf-Road-Woman. She accompanied the warriors to take care of her husband, Black Coyote, and her brother, Chief Comes-in-Sight. At a crucial moment in the battle, her brother's horse was killed. Chief Comes-in-Sight stood by his dead horse and continued to fight bravely as soldiers began to surround him. Upon seeing her brother in such grave danger, Buffalo-Calf-Road-Woman gave the Cheyenne war cry and rushed to save him. She galloped past the surprised soldiers and reached for her brother, who leaped onto the back of her horse. Together they raced to safety. Her brave deed so impressed everyone that for a few minutes the fighting stopped. The Indians filled the air with war cries. Some of the soldiers tossed their caps into the air and cheered. To this day, the Cheyenne call the engagement the Battle Where the Girl Saved Her Brother.

A week after the **Battle of the Rosebud**, another group of soldiers led by the famous George Armstrong Custer came to attack the Lakota, the Cheyenne, and the Arapaho along the Little Bighorn River in eastern Montana. Although Custer's attack on June 25, 1876, surprised the Indians, they fought bravely in defense of their families and their homeland. It was a great victory for the Indians that day. They killed Custer and more than 200 of his soldiers in what is often called "Custer's Last Stand." One of the bravest Indians who died that day was a young warrior named Limberbones. He was an ancestor of Dennis Limberhand, one of the authors of this book.

The defeat embarrassed the U.S. Army, which was determined then to punish all the Indians who fought at Little Bighorn. Within a year most of the Indians who had been with Sitting Bull were either on reservations or hiding in Canada. The Northern Cheyenne were taken prisoner and sent away to live in Indian Territory in Oklahoma with their southern relatives.

After many unsuccessful attempts to convince the United States government that they did not want to live in the hot climate, starving conditions, and disease in Oklahoma, the Northern Cheyenne, under chiefs Dull Knife and Little Wolf, escaped on foot. During their trek from Oklahoma to their Montana homeland, several women, children, and warriors lost their lives, but some managed to travel on. When they got near Fort Robinson, Nebraska, they split into two groups. One group, under the leadership of Little Wolf, hid in the hills. The other group, under Dull Knife, mostly elders, women, and children, decided to surrender at Fort

Two Cheyenne chiefs and heroes, Little Wolf (standing) and Dull Knife (seated). They were photographed before 1877 by William Henry Jackson, a painter and early photographer of the West.

The Southern Cheyenne were moved to Oklahoma in about 1870, but Northern Cheyenne resisted until they were forced to join the Southern group after 1876. The Northern Cheyenne escaped from Oklahoma, but some were killed in the attempt or were soon recaptured. Some, however, did make the trip all the way to either Nebraska or the homelands in Wyoming and Montana.

Robinson, expecting to receive permission to return to the North to their own homeland. Instead, the soldiers at the fort locked the Cheyenne in a barracks. Although it was in the coldest part of the winter, the Cheyenne prisoners tried to escape, but most were shot and killed during the attempt.

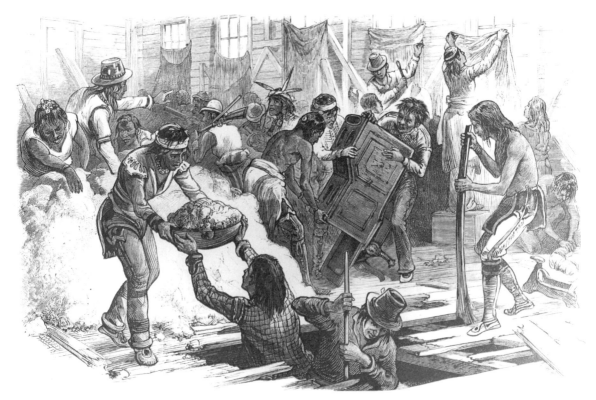

Having escaped on foot from forced relocation in Oklahoma, one group of Northern Cheyenne under Dull Knife surrendered at Fort Robinson, Nebraska. This illustration shows them preparing to escape from that fort. Most were killed in the attempt.

Following this tragedy, the government finally agreed to let the Northern Cheyenne have a homeland in Montana again. In 1884 the Northern Cheyenne were given expanded lands for their Montana reservation, where many still live today.

When this time of troubles passed, the tribe slowly began to grow. According to a census taken in 1904, the Northern Cheyenne had approximately 1,400 tribal members. The Southern Cheyenne had approximately 1,900. Although many troubles lay ahead, the tribes continued to grow. Currently the Northern Cheyenne have about 8,000 members, and the Southern Cheyenne and Arapaho number about 6,500.

Way of Life

As nomads, the Cheyenne economy or way of life centered on the buffalo. At first, the Cheyenne hunted these massive creatures by chasing them over cliffs called "buffalo jumps." After acquiring horses in the 18th century, Cheyenne men usually hunted them from horseback using spears and arrows. The meat of the buffalo provided the Cheyenne with much of their food. The hides were made into blankets and covers for their tents, which were called **tipis** (tepees). The bones, hooves, and horns became tools, cups, and rattles. The tails became fly-swatters. The Cheyenne used every part of the buffalo, wasting nothing. Even the manure, called "buffalo chips," was often used instead of wood to make campfires.

The Cheyenne always followed the migrating buffalo herds. Each summer and fall the tribe would kill enough buffalo to feed the people during the cold winters. Each year they killed enough buffalo to obtain fresh hides needed to make robes, new tipi covers, and other necessary items.

A hide scraper (above) was made from animal bone. A powder horn (left) was attached to a buckskin pouch and ornamented with beadwork. The long buckskin strap is covered with red flannel, perhaps received in trade.

Food

Besides the buffalo, the Cheyenne diet consisted of elk, deer, antelope, and other small animals. The Cheyenne also ate plums, turnips, wild berries, chokecherries, herbs, roots, and other plants, but they preferred meat. A favorite and nutritious food was pemmican. It was like the modern dehydrated food that campers use today. Pemmican was made from dried meat that was first pounded with a stone hammer. The meat was then mixed with melted animal fat and paste made from berries. Pemmican did not spoil easily and could be eaten even years after it was made. It was often stored in a folded rawhide container called a **parfleche**.

A Cheyenne parfleche (pouch) made from bison hide.

Housing

Tipis, or lodges, were ideal houses for the nomadic Cheyenne. They were made of buffalo skins stretched over poles made from lodgepole pine trees. The cone-shaped tents were easy to make, simple to erect, and could be folded into compact bundles. Tipis were made in various sizes depending upon the number of people living in them. They were usually between 12 and 16 feet (3.6 and 5 m) across at the base and were made from 8 to 12 buffalo skins carefully tanned and sewn tightly together.

While the Cheyenne were still free, they lived in tipi villages that could be moved easily. This camp was pitched in about 1870.

The fireplace was in the center of the lodge directly beneath a smoke hole. Two flaps covered the smoke hole. The hole could be opened or closed by means of two long poles that fit into a buffalo ear sewn into the edge of each flap.

There were strict rules for visiting a family in its tipi, and items in the tipi were carefully arranged. The head of the household sat opposite the door. Around the inside were beds made from buffalo robes and pillows stuffed with fur and the floss from cottonwood trees. Furniture was backrests made from willow sticks. Pouches and parfleches were used for storage.

Like most other aspects of Indian life, the tipi had spiritual importance. The doorways always faced east toward the rising sun. The floor represented the earth, and the walls represented the sky. The poles were the trails from earth to the Spirit World.

Women were responsible for maintaining the household, and they also organized all of the camp moves. Everything a Cheyenne family owned was lightweight and easy to pack. Most of the baggage was packed on a **travois**. It was like a wagon without wheels. Travois were made by tying

A Cheyenne baby carrier (above) was used in about 1885. With a horsedrawn travois (left) made of lodgepole pines, a family— mother, daughters, baby, and all—could move their possessions quickly.

Way of Life   23

two tipi poles together and laying them across the neck and shoulders of a horse. The opposite ends were held together by cross-sticks. The cover from the tipi was placed on the travois. It was used as a large bed by little children and elders, and also for carrying belongings.

Clothing

Women made clothing for everyone from the hides of deer, elk, and buffalo. They wore buckskin dresses, skirts and capes, and short leggings. The men wore shirts, **breechcloths**, and high leggings. Men and women wore moccasins, which were decorated with beads in various designs. Children were dressed much like adults. The Cheyenne also wore buffalo robes in colder weather. They decorated their clothing with objects found in nature. Among these were porcupine quills, shells, ferns, and grasses dyed with colors made from natural materials, such as plants, dirt, and minerals. By 1800, the Cheyenne began decorating their clothes with glass beads, coins, and other objects they received by trading with Europeans.

A rare and beautiful girl's dress was made of buckskin, with buckskin fringe. It was decorated with seashells. The shells came originally from the Pacific Ocean and were carried far inland by traders.

Arts and Crafts

Beadwork and quillwork were important crafts for the Cheyenne. Most of their designs were geometric. They also painted rawhide articles such as tipis, robes, and shields that protected warriors in battle. Plains Indians were also known for their carving skills. They carved stone pipes and beautiful wooden flutes. Feathers symbolized medicine and strength. Feathers were used to decorate shields, banners, shirts, and worn in men's hair. Large, circular bustles of feathers were popular for wear when **powwow** dancing.

A Cheyenne girl (above left) wears finely braided hair decorations as part of her powwow dress at the St. Labre Indian School.

A panther skin (left) had scenes of great events painted by Yellow Nose.

A spear (right) was decorated with feathers.

Medicine

There is a real difference between the Indian meaning of medicine and the modern definition of medical practice. Indians believed that there must be a balance or harmony within nature. They believed that it was a person's job to help keep that balance. If people did not help keep the balance, illness, disease, famine, or disaster would follow. When those evils of imbalance appeared, medicine men performed special ceremonies to heal the wounded or cure illnesses. Medicine men might also use special herbs and other natural remedies to help with cures. Warriors carried special medicine items to ward off evil and bad spirits. These medicine-bearing items could be rocks, plant roots, or parts of animals or birds.

Teaching students the medical benefits of plants, a late elder of the Northern Cheyenne Reservation, William Tall Bull, passed along practical knowledge, oral history, and many traditions.

Spiritual Life

The Cheyenne people, like most Indians of the Plains, believed that spiritual powers were an important part of their life. All of nature, even objects that are not alive, could have sacred powers that came from the Creator. The Cheyenne believed that all powers came from **Maheo**, the Great Spirit. Ceremonial dances and rituals, such as "taking a sweat" in a sweat lodge filled with steaming hot rocks, smoking the pipe, and possessing **medicine bundles**, were important elements of the Cheyenne way of life. They were so important that each Cheyenne considered his or her existence inseparable from the spiritual way of life.

According to legend, the culture hero **Sweet Medicine** traveled to **Bear Butte** in the Black Hills of present-day South Dakota. Bear Butte remains a very sacred place to the Cheyenne people. They believe that special supernatural powers come to the Cheyenne from this mountain. It was there that the Creator gave Sweet Medicine the **Sacred Arrows**. These arrows are still held today by the Southern Cheyenne in Oklahoma. The other sacred object, the **Sacred Buffalo Hat**, given to the Cheyenne, is with the Northern Cheyenne in Montana. The keepers of the Sacred Arrows and the Sacred Buffalo Hat are very important men indeed.

The tipi of Issiwun held the Sacred Buffalo Hat of the Northern Cheyennes in 1906. At the top of the tipi poles is Nimhoyah, or sacred "turner," which turns away sickness and disease. The Sacred Buffalo Hat remains very important in Cheyenne life.

27

The day before the Battle of the Little Bighorn, Custer's troops passed this sandstone formation, known as Deer Medicine Rock. Ancient drawings cover the rock. This one (left) is a symbol of the Cheyenne. Here, too, the Lakota chief Sitting Bull had a vision that the soldiers would fall. And soon after, they did.

During the summer encampment, a renewal ceremony called the Sun Dance took place and still does today. The ceremony usually lasts four or five days. A special lodge is built and blessed before the Sun Dance Ceremony. Participation at the renewal ceremony is important for all tribal members. If one Cheyenne had killed another, he was banned from participating in the ceremony and was sent four rivers away during the time of the ceremony. Young men sacrifice by not eating or drinking during this time. One of the most important persons in the ceremony is a woman who holds a sacred office. Families also are important in preparing the food and assisting the dancers with camp preparation.

Animals are a central element of the Cheyenne religion. The **eagle** is a symbol of spiritual strength and power. It is believed to be a messenger to the Creator. The **bear** is also sacred. It is thought to bring good fortune. A symbol of independence as well, the bear is considered to be a Cheyenne relative—similar to an uncle.

Family Life

To the Cheyenne people, the family and the extended family make up the most important social unit, as do the smaller band and the larger overall tribe or nation. In the old days, bands lived away from one another but came together for special occasions and in times of need.

Courtship and Marriage

Marriage was (and is) sacred to the Cheyenne, whose women were known for their purity and desired as wives. Marriages were often arranged, but sometimes young men and women fell in love and ran away to get married. Women who were captured from other tribes sometimes married Cheyenne men. A man who could afford it sometimes had more than one wife, and they all lived together as one family.

This photograph, taken in 1913, was labeled "Cheyenne belles." And, indeed, these young women would have been sought after by young men wanting to marry them. Sometimes a man could even afford more than one wife.

Courting was a long process. Family members arranged dates. A young man dated his bride-to-be for an extended period of time. Women covered most of their bodies with a robe or blanket, and a man could only see her face. Mothers, grand-

Florence Whiteman, the last woman warrior of the Northern Cheyennes, is also the last Cheyenne given to her husband for the bride price of four horses. She was wed in 1943 at age 15. (When widowed, Florence picked her own second husband.)

mothers, or aunts usually accompanied young women when they went to meet a man. If a man did not have someone to arrange a meeting, he might wait for hours along a path that a woman was known to travel just to get a glimpse of her. If she did not want to speak to him, she would look away and pretend not to see him. However, if she liked him, she would stop and talk, but never about love or marriage. Finally, if they decided to marry, both fathers, or heads of family, would meet, and the man's family would offer gifts to the woman's family. A husband usually went to live with or near his wife's family. However, by custom his mother-in-law could not look at or speak to him. She had to communicate through her daughter or a third person.

Family

The larger family unit camped together, although they might live in several lodges. Great-grandparents, grandparents, un-married brothers and sisters, parents, and children all lived together in one family group. Women claimed ownership of the tipis and household possessions. They were in charge of making the clothing and feeding the family. Women also ran the house-hold and supervised the family moves. Men supplied the food

Northern Cheyenne Laban Little Wolf, nephew of Little Wolf, posed in front of his tipi with his family. He fought at the Battle of the Little Bighorn. Relatives of Laban Little Wolf still reside on the Cheyenne Reservation in Montana.

by fishing and hunting for meat. They also provided defense and protection for the family. They were in charge of the horse herds and kept a lookout for enemies.

On cold winter nights, the family sat around the fire while the elders told myths and stories. The favorite stories were of brave war deeds, spiritual happenings, and tales of animals such as wolves, who were symbols of warriors. These stories provided instruction for young boys in the ways of the warrior and their duties to protect and care for people. Children were encouraged to respect moral values and to avoid greed and irresponsibility. They were also taught to respect their elders. The elders, in turn, taught the children songs and instructed them in the cultural values of the tribe.

Utah Two Two, dressed like many teenagers today, stares into a campfire, as the moon rises above the Northern Cheyenne Reservation.

Young boys played hunting games. They learned to ride horses and to hunt rabbits and birds. Also they were taught to read signs of nature so they could become good trackers and hunters. Young boys often accompanied hunting and war parties. Their job was to hold horses, carry moccasins and supplies, gather firewood, and do other tasks as needed around the camps.

Grandmothers made deerskin dolls for the girls and taught them how to do beadwork and quilling. By helping their mothers, girls learned how to tan hides, to pick berries, and to cook. To prepare their daughters for building lodges, mothers built small models that were used to instruct them in the proper way to set up a tipi cover and stake it to the ground.

Girls and boys learned social skills such as dancing and the care of the home and camp. They also learned to develop their survival skills. Children were encouraged to play running and hunting games in order to increase their speed and strength. They had footraces and horse races. Girls played with toy tipis and with deerskin dolls. When snow covered the ground,

It may be the same in all cultures and in all times from ancient to modern. At some point in life, many girls like to play with dolls and play house. These Cheyenne girls did it their own way, with dolls and tipis.

fathers made sleds for their children out of buffalo ribs. As they were used, the bones became smoother than modern steel sled runners.

Brothers and sisters were very close and took care of one another. However, once grown up, brothers and sisters kept their distance from each other and often spoke through a third person. This is not necessarily true today.

Most children are given two names—a Cheyenne name and an English name. The elders, usually grandmothers, conduct name-giving ceremonies. A gift-giving and a feast are held in honor of this special event. During conversations among inter-tribal groups, the Cheyenne prefer to be identified as Northern Cheyenne or Southern Cheyenne. When addressing a mixed group of different tribes, it is appropriate to call them American Indians or Native Americans. When greeting people, Cheyenne shake hands even before an introduction is made.

Tribal Society

Traditionally, the Cheyenne had 44 chiefs. The chiefs formed the **council** and governed the tribe. Five of them were headmen who assumed the leadership roles for the council. The rest were chiefs who represented the different family groups or bands. The council decided major tribal policy and made alliances and war decisions involving other tribes or the United States government. However, the chiefs' council seldom arranged military strategy or made day-to-day decisions. These were usually left to the military societies.

The role of the tribal chiefs was honorary. They had little authority, but their advice was well respected. Appointed for their bravery, character, wisdom, and calm, they were also expected to be fair, generous, and courageous. Their main job was to preserve the peace by settling disputes and differences.

Tribal chiefs, like Two Moon, led by their character and wisdom, not by force of power.

Military Societies

In some respects military societies among the Cheyenne were similar to units in a modern army, but they were also like social clubs. Members met to plan battles, to organize ceremonial functions, to replace tribal leaders, and to help families in times of hardship. Each society had its own rituals, sacred objects, and ways. The best known of these military societies was the "Hotamitanio" or "**Dog Soldiers**." Dog Soldiers were fearless warriors who played an important part in battles against enemy tribes and the United States Army during the Indian wars of the 1860s and 1870s. Dog Soldiers led the warriors into battle, and, when the tribe moved camp, they formed the rear guard. They maintained law and order and disciplined those who violated tribal law.

Other military societies included the "Kit Fox," "Elkhorn Scrapers," "Bowstring," and "Crazy Dogs." Another group called the "Contraries" were individuals who had special ways and beliefs which were usually opposite of what others did. This society system is still intact today. Some Cheyenne women could join warrior societies. But most belonged to their own organizations, such as "The Quillers' Society," whose members made beautiful clothing embroidered with porcupine quills.

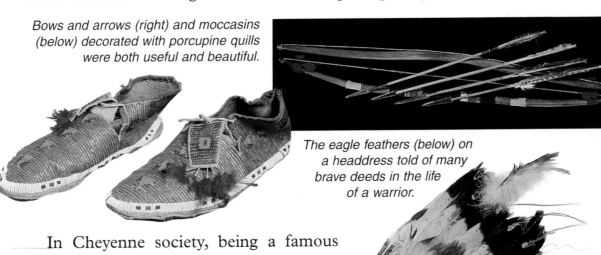

Bows and arrows (right) and moccasins (below) decorated with porcupine quills were both useful and beautiful.

The eagle feathers (below) on a headdress told of many brave deeds in the life of a warrior.

In Cheyenne society, being a famous warrior was like being a star athlete on a football or basketball team today. Warriors earned special honors for brave deeds like touching an enemy in battle or sneaking into an enemy camp at night and capturing a horse. These brave deeds were called coups, a French word meaning "triumph."

Sometimes a warrior would receive an eagle feather for a successful coup. Great warriors sometimes got so many eagle feathers they would make a war bonnet to wear in battle. Their war bonnets identified them as great fighters, and their enemies would try even harder to catch them.

Government

Today, the governing body on the Northern Cheyenne reservation is the Tribal Council. Representatives on the council are elected by adults who vote in five districts. Tribal members elect the tribal president and vice president. The Northern Cheyenne nation has its own legal system, and the people elect tribal judges. The tribe administers a full set of service agencies dedicated to finance, education, community health, and natural resources. The Southern Cheyenne and Arapaho nation are governed in a similar way, with equal representation from each nation.

Today's Tribal Council of the Northern Cheyenne has a Capitol Building to work from. They serve people from respected elders to young boys on bikes with a puppy to tend.

Contemporary Life

Members of the Cheyenne tribes today live in two different locations. The Northern Cheyenne, numbering approximately 8,000, live on the Northern Cheyenne Reservation in southeastern Montana, mainly near the town Lame Deer, while the Southern Cheyenne have joint lands with the Arapaho and are located near Concho, Oklahoma.

The Northern Cheyenne Reservation covers 460,000 acres (186,200 ha) of land. Much of the land is devoted to cattle ranching, farming, and the production of timber products. The

Northern Cheyenne battlegrounds and locations of important sites are shown in the map on the left. Southern Cheyenne places of interest are scattered over western Oklahoma (shown at right).

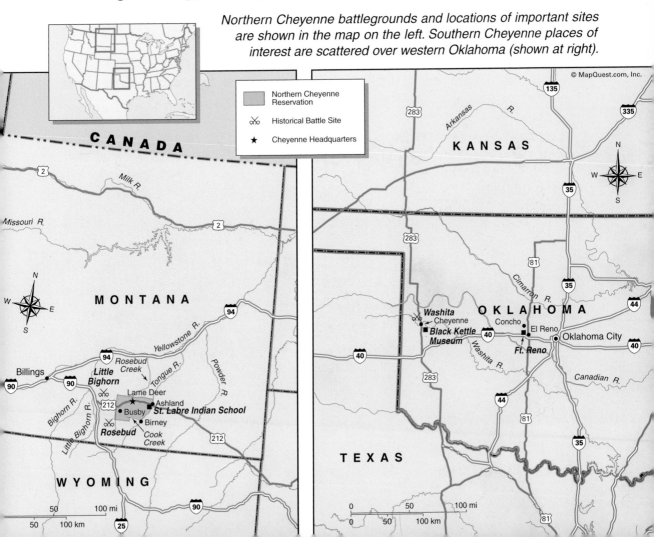

© MapQuest.com, Inc.

Cheyenne also maintain a herd of 100–200 buffalo that are used primarily for ceremonial purposes. When a buffalo is killed for a ceremony, it is butchered in the traditional way. The buffalo's tongue and the hump on its back are considered choice parts for eating. Bones, hides, hooves, and horns are used either for ceremonies or for tools or utensils.

Although there is potential for oil and gas drilling on the reservation, the tribe does not have any producing wells. Vast deposits of coal underlie reservation land. At one time there were plans for mining the coal, but the tribe canceled its leases with the coal companies. Respect for the land and the traditions surrounding it were more important than the money oil or coal might produce.

The major employers on the reservation are the Tribe, the Bureau of Indian Affairs, the Indian Health Services, the St. Labre Indian School, and local energy companies. Each summer many young Cheyenne men and women work fighting

Young Justin Whiteman guides a trio of ponies during a parade that celebrated Native American culture at the St. Labre Indian School in Ashland, Montana.

forest fires. Other seasonal jobs are available in construction, carpentry, road building, and farm and ranch work.

The Cheyenne operate a small casino and a bingo hall located in Lame Deer, Montana. The tribe owns convenience stores and gas stations on the reservation. A sawmill operation in Ashland, Montana, and various other small business operations employ people on the reservation today.

Woodsie King (above) a new high school graduate, gives the universal "thumbs up" sign. Forest Oldman (below) wears the dance outfit of a traditional warrior during a powwow at St. Labre.

Tribal members live in several major communities. Lame Deer is the capital of the reservation and location of the tribal headquarters. Busby is the home of the White River Cheyenne. Others live in Ashland, which is also the location of the St. Labre Indian School. Birney, a traditional village located on the Tongue River, marks the southern boundary of the reservation.

Children attend school on the reservation or in nearby public schools. Three elementary schools and three high schools are located on the reservation. Children learn reading, writing, and other familiar school subjects such as English, history, science, and mathematics. There has also been a renewal of teaching of the Cheyenne language to the young both in school and at home. **Bilingual** teaching is offered in the schools. The students also study their Cheyenne heritage and history. At Dull Knife Memorial College, there is a heavy emphasis on learning the traditional Cheyenne culture and language, as well as on the regular academic curriculum.

St. Labre Indian School students throw handmade arrows through a hoop. This game has been passed on for generations on the Northern Cheyenne Reservation.

The Cheyenne celebrate an annual powwow over the Fourth of July during which they dance, play stick games, and do other traditional activities. A Sun Dance, a religious ceremony of fasting, ceremonial singing and dancing, and purification, is also held yearly. Before the Sun Dance, the Southern Cheyenne and Southern Arapaho conduct the Arrow Ceremony called "New Life Lodge."

Many families have their own sweat lodge, which they use on a regular basis. When in the sweat lodge, the Cheyenne communicate with the spiritual world.

Young people participate in sports, watch videos, play video games, use computers, and drive around in cars much like teenagers do everywhere else in the United States. A boys and girls club active on the reservation provides youth activities and cultural awareness activities.

Senator Ben Nighthorse Campbell, a Colorado Republican, is a Northern Cheyenne and the only Native American

Senator Ben Nighthorse Campbell in full traditional dress with feathered headdress, buckskins, beadwork, and facepaint helps celebrate the 1999 groundbreaking in Washington, D.C., of the Smithsonian Institution's National Museum of the American Indian.

in the United States Congress. His great-grandfather, Black Horse, fought at the Battle of the Little Bighorn. Senator Campbell did not grow up on the reservation, but he has many relatives there. He goes back to the "rez" a couple of times a year for spiritual renewal and to visit family and friends. He is committed to his native Cheyenne culture.

The Northern Cheyenne and Southern Cheyenne tribes today experience many of the same problems reflected in American society. Poverty, drug and alcohol problems, substandard housing, lack of medical care, and high unemployment are major concerns on the reservation. The Cheyenne are working hard to overcome racism and prejudice. They want to contribute to solving their own problems. The majority of Cheyenne have adapted to living in both worlds, the white world and the Indian world. They want to share their culture and traditions. If you wish to visit the Northern Cheyenne Reservation today you are welcome to do so.

Cheyenne Recipe

Wild Chokecherry Pudding

(from Helen Highwalker, 80-year-old aunt of author Dennis Limberhand)

Long ago every woman had a hollowed stone and stone pounder. The cherries were put into an earthen bowl and pounded a few at a time. Then a cloth was spread out on a table in the sun. Patties were made, then dried in the sun, and packed into a sack. Today Cheyennes use electric meat grinders or freeze freshly picked cherries.

Adult supervision is required.

6 cups chokecherries (In August choke-
    cherries are ready to pick. Be sure to
    leave the stems on while picking.)
2 quarts water
1 cup flour
cold water
4-inch square vegetable shortening
sugar

This is a cultivated chokecherry bush. The ones found in the wild may not have berries in such large clusters.

1. Wash the cherries in cold water.

2. Place the cherries in a saucepan with 2 quarts water and cook until mushy.

3. Mix 1 cup of flour in cold water to the consistency of gravy.

4. While cherries cook, strain flour mixture into the hot cherries.

5. Boil until thickened, stirring constantly.

6. Put a 4-inch square of vegetable shortening into the cherry mixture.

7. Sweeten to taste. (Don't add sugar until berries are done.)

Cheyenne Game

The "Hand or Stick Game" is a guessing game. There are two sides. Each side, or team, has ten sticks. Each side also has an elk's tooth or a marked stone. A team member places the tooth or marked stone in one hand. The other team has to guess which hand the player is holding it in. If the guessing team makes a wrong choice, that team has to give up one of its sticks. The object of the game is for one team to win all the sticks. "Hand" games are still popular among Indian peoples.

Cheyenne Chronology

Before 1700	Cheyennes live as woodland farmers in what is now Wisconsin and Minnesota.
c. 1680	Cheyennes meet white men for the first time in the person of French explorer Robert de La Salle and his party.
c. 1700	Cheyennes are driven from lands east of the Mississippi River by their enemies, the Ojibwa and the Assiniboin.
1700s	Cheyennes adopt the plains style of hunting buffalo from horseback as they migrate west toward the Black Hills of the Dakotas.
1804	Cheyennes meet the explorers Meriwether Lewis and William Clark.
Early 1800s	Many white people begin to travel through Cheyenne country.
1832	Cheyennes divide into two groups. One, called the Northern, settles near the headwaters of the Platte River. The other, called the Southern, settles near the upper Arkansas River.
1851	The Southern Cheyenne and the Arapaho sign a treaty with the United States to guarantee safe passage of white settlers who were moving west.
1856	An unjust killing near Fort Kearney, Nebraska, begins 20 years of war with the U.S. Army.
1864	The village of Chief Black Kettle at Sand Creek is attacked by the U.S. Army.
1868	Black Kettle's village at Washita is attacked again— by George Armstrong Custer's troops.
1876	Cheyennes, with Lakota Sioux and Arapaho allies, defeat and destroy Lt. Colonel Custer and his troops at the Battle of the Little Bighorn.
1884	After bitter defeats and imprisonment, Northern Cheyenne are given land in Montana for a reservation.

1900s	Cheyennes face hard times, low employment, and lack of education. They continue to survive and grow in numbers, confidence, and cultural pride, although many still live in poverty.
1924	Passage of the Indian Citizen Act which grants U.S. citizenship to all Indians.
1925	Passage of Reorganization Act. It provides for tribal self-government, restoration of lands, and permitting Indians to once again practice their traditional cultures.
1926	Passage of Senate Joint Resolution guaranteeing religious freedom to all Native Americans.
1992	Tribal member Ben Nighthorse Campbell is elected to the U.S. Senate from Colorado. He is the only Native American in either the House of Representatives or the Senate.

Coauthor Dennis Limberhand stands in front of Deer Medicine Rock, still sacred to the Cheyenne.

Glossary

Assiniboin (uh-SIN-uh-BOYN) Traditional enemies of the Cheyenne.

Battle of the Rosebud Battle in Montana in which Cheyenne and Lakota Sioux battled the U.S. Army. This occurred ten days before the Battle of the Little Bighorn.

Bear An animal that is a symbol of strength.

Bear Butte A mountain in South Dakota. It is believed by Cheyenne to be a place of supernatural power.

Bilingual Having the ability to speak two languages.

Breechcloth Simple garment worn by men from the waist to the upper thigh.

Council Cheyenne chiefs that governed the tribe.

Dog Soldiers Special unit of a fearless Cheyenne warrior society.

Eagle A spirit messenger, the bird that is a symbol of independence.

Maheo (mah-HEE-oh) The Creator, a source of spiritual power to the Cheyenne.

Medicine bundle Items used for ceremonial and spiritual purposes.

Ojibwa (oh-JIB-way) Indian nation that destroyed early Cheyenne settlements.

Parfleche (PAR-flesh) A rawhide bag or case used for storage.

Powwow An Indian cultural gathering and dance celebration.

Reservation Land set aside by U.S. Government for tribal or other use.

Sacred Arrows Source of spiritual power for Cheyenne.

Sacred Buffalo Hat Source of spiritual power for Cheyenne.

Sweet Medicine A Cheyenne prophet hero.

Tipi (TEE-pee) A cone-shaped structure supported by poles and covered with animal skins.

Travois (tra-VOY) Poles tied to a horse to carry possessions.

Further Reading

Eder, Jeanne Oyawin. *The Dakota Sioux*. Austin, TX: Raintree Steck-Vaughn Publishers, 2000.

Henry, Christopher E. *Ben Nighthorse Campbell: Cheyenne Chief and U.S. Senator*. Broomall, PA: Chelsea House, 1994.

Meli, Franco. *A Cheyenne*. Minneapolis: Runestone Press, 1999.

Sheve, Virginia Driving Hawk. *The Cheyennes: A First Americans Book*. New York: Holiday House, 1996.

Viola, Herman J. *It Is a Good Day to Die: Indian Eyewitnesses Tell the Story of the Battle of the Little Bighorn*. New York: Crown Publishers, 1998.

Viola, Herman J. *North American Indians: An Introduction to the Lives of America's Native Peoples, From the Inuit of the Arctic to the Zuni of the Southwest*. New York: Crown Publishers, 1996.

Sources

Bancroft-Hunt, Norman. *The Indians of the Great Plains*. London: Little, Brown & Co., 1981.

Editors of Time-Life Books. *The Buffalo Hunters* (The American Indian). Alexandria, VA: 1993.

Editors of Time-Life Books. *War for the Plains* (The American Indian). Alexandria, VA: 1994.

Erdoes, Richard, and Alfonso Ortiz, eds. *American Indian Myths and Legends*. New York: Pantheon Books, 1984.

Griffin-Pierce, Trudy. *The Encyclopedia of Native America*. New York: Viking, 1995.

National Museum of the American Indian, George Gustav Heye Center, Alexander Hamilton U.S. Custom House, New York City, NY.

Northern Cheyenne Tribal Center, P.O. Box 128, Lame Deer, Montana 59043, (406) 477-6285, website: www.ncheyenne.net, http://members.xoom.com/eaglewing/

The Cheyenne and Arapaho Tribes of Oklahoma, 100 Red Moon Circle, Concho, Oklahoma 73022, (405) 262-0345, website: www.cheyenne-arapaho.nsn.us/

Index

Numbers in italics indicate illustration or map.